I'm a Clinician NOT A Magician

How to Create Rapid Change in Your Mental Health and Happiness.

Dr. Mary Burkhead Spencer
ImaClinicianNotaMagician.com

I'm a Clinician NOT a Magician

is a common sense guide on how to create rapid change in your mental health and happiness.

Dr. Mary Burkhead Spencer

Copyright © 2021 Dr. Mary Burkhead Spencer

All rights reserved. No part of this publication may be reproduced, distributed, or transmitted in any form or by any means, including photocopying, recording, or other electronic or mechanical methods, without the prior written permission from the author, except in the case of brief quotations embodied in critical reviews and certain other non-commercial uses permitted by copyright law.

First Printing: April 2021

www.ImaClinicianNotaMagician.com

ISBN# 978-1-7370361-0-4

Why Read This Book

There is no smarter way to live your life and make significant changes than by not repeating past behaviors. **Viktor Frankl** was imprisoned in a Nazi concentration camp. "Everything can be taken from a man but one thing," **Frankl** wrote in his book *A Man's Search for Ultimate Meaning*, "the last of the human freedoms – to choose one's attitude in any given set of circumstances, to choose one's own way." Joshua instructed his people, "Choose you this day whom you will serve."

When Ted Bundy was thirteen years old, he found filthy magazines in the trash near where he lived. While looking through them, he became captivated. His lust to read about torture and violence grew into an addiction. After a while, just reading them and pleasuring himself was not enough and he had to start committing the acts in order to climax. Imagine if had just thrown them in the fire instead. He might have saved himself from evil. We ALL face crossroads and choices between good and evil, smart and stupid, life and death.

Are you ready to make better choices?

Do you want to feel empowered and have a meaningful life?

This book will help you learn to take the time and find the wisdom to make better choices. Whether large or small, choices direct the pathway of our life. Life is about choices. You chose your choices. You don't get to choose your consequences.

Just ask Ted Bundy.

TO

Succeed

IN LIFE, YOU NEED THREE THINGS

A wishbone, a backbone, and a funnybone.

-REBA MCINTIRE

Written by a Leading Expert in Making Better Life Choices

Dr. Mary Burkhead Spencer is a Licensed Professional Counselor with a PhD in Psychology. She has had her own Private Practice for many years. She has been published in The Encyclopedia of Human Services and Diversity by Linwood H. Cousins. She graduated Valedictorian from Haltom High School and went on to obtain a Bachelor's in Business from LeTourneau University, a Master's in Counseling from Argosy University, and a PhD in Psychology from Walden University. Her dissertation explores "Where Women Who Were Abandoned by Their Father's Prior to the Age of Eighteen Are Today in Their Intimate Romantic Relationships." Basically, exploring how much a father figure influences a girl's relationship success as an adult. She is also an ICBCH Certified Professional Hypnotherapist. She is married to her high school sweetheart and they have two amazing sons, amazing daughters in law, and six amazing grandchildren!

Table of Contents

CHAPTER ONE : I'm a Clinician, not a Magician..................1

CHAPTER TWO : Choices. Life's about 'em. 10

CHAPTER THREE : So Simple a Child Can Do It! Choices. Life's about 'em. 15

CHAPTER FOUR : Stop Looking in the Rear-View Mirror When You Should be Focused on the Road Ahead 21

CHAPTER FIVE : Depression is anger turned inward. Anger is a response to being hurt. 25

CHAPTER SIX : ANXIETY 32

CHAPTER SEVEN : BE PREPARED.......................................41

CHAPTER EIGHT: Do Not Let People Live Rent Free in Your Head. Evict Them..47

CHAPTER NINE : Work 52

CHAPTER TEN : Weight Loss...62

CHAPTER ELEVEN : RELATIONSHIPS 73

CHAPTER TWELVE : Coffee, potatoes, and eggs................80

CHAPTER THIRTEEN : My thoughts for a penny. 82

CHAPTER FOURTEEN : The Road......................................86

ONE

I'm a Clinician, not a Magician.

My writer guru friend said to start with how you know the promise you're about to make is real.

Here's the promise: Life's about choices. You choose your choices. You don't get to choose your consequences. **BAM! Nailed it!**

People come to me for therapy and to help them have a better life. What some really want is presto chango your life is fixed. They have cheated on their husband and they want to bring him in and me **make** him come back home. They have been arrested for drunk driving and they want me to write them a letter to the court explaining they have attended therapy and get them out of trouble. They want me to inform their college that they have given up drugs so they do not get kicked out of college. They want to have a hypnotherapy session with me for weight loss and wake up tomorrow thin. **I'm a Clinician, NOT a Magician.**

Here's my thesis. If you continue to read this book, your life experiences will improve as you learn to mindfully make better choices. When at a crossroad, ask yourself: Is this something I will be glad I did or something that I will wish I had not done? Is my desired choice morally sound? If my child were me, would I recommend they do this or not do this? Would you suggest your son or daughter drink and drive? Of course not. I tell my clients, if you choose to drink and drive and you go to prison instead of college, that's on you. YOU CHOSE. You chose to drink. You chose to drive. You once were lost but now you're found.

I once was introduced to a man with no arms and no legs and yet he was making a profound difference in the lives of others, especially teenagers. Even now he travels the world spreading hope. He has a wife and children. He runs an organization called Life Without Limbs (lifewithoutlimbs.org). Anyone who has ever watched him, leaves inspired. He has an Australian accent and a jolly good sense of humor. He also has a prison ministry.

He could have been pitiful, but he chooses to be powerful.

As a therapist, I've heard all the excuses. So, you come from a family of alcoholics. Stop with the victimhood. If you come from a family of alcoholics, don't take that first drink. It's not worth the risk. Someone needs to break the cycle and it might as well be you. End the "name it and claim it" attitude. As you continue to read the pages of this book you will find the strength and focus and courage to cultivate and grow more sound reasoning skills and become the author of your own life as best you can. There are somethings in life we have no control over. It's what we do with the cards we are dealt.

This doesn't mean we should go through life way overthinking everything. Let's be reasonable.

A client was having trouble in his marriage. At work he has a very important "think fast on your feet to save lives" job. So, he barks orders that must be followed because it is the nature of saving lives. While this makes him a superstar at work, barking orders at home (while it comes naturally) is not well received. In therapy we devised a plan such that when he gets mad and frustrated at home and he feels like barking orders, he looks at his watch and he notes the time. He gives himself 10 minutes before he says anything. After the 10 minutes, he thinks about it again and usually realizes it really does not matter and does not even need to be said. At this point, after the 10 minutes have passed, he has never felt he should say anything, and his home life is much better.

Throughout my therapy practice I have seen people of all ages. Choices usually always come up. If you choose to be mean to your sister and your mother takes away your favorite toy, that was your choice. Mom told you that if you did it again, she was going to take it away and you did it again. If mom did not take it away like she said she would, then she would be a liar. So now you know mom's not kidding so the choice is yours – disobey and lose your toy or obey and get to keep it. Honestly, the younger a person can learn this, the better off their life will be.

If you choose to cheat on your spouse, you may find that fifteen minutes of euphoria caused you a lifetime of trouble.

As a child listening to grown-ups talk, I realized I needed to be proactive in my own choices.

I'm going to tell you a story from my own personal experiences. I'm the little red-haired girl that was born to older parents. My dad was the 11th of 13 children and my mother was the 5th of 7 children. I am of mostly Irish descent. My mother was 41 years old and my father was 51 years old when I was born. Prior to my birth, my father had decided to become semi-retired and have my mother get a part time job so he could go fishing more. My mother hated her job, so she prayed. I should state here that my mother took her walk with Christ very seriously. She prayed and asked God to "make David the hardworking man he'd always been." My mother became quite sickly and weak. She started eating more salt thinking that she had a salt deficiency. She finally went to the doctor and he told her, "Stop with the salt and you're pregnant." To which she responded, "No." He shrugged. "I'm 40 years old and I usually only have one period a year." He shrugged again. Needless to say, my dad was surprised and terrified. He told my mom that he was too old and would never live to see the baby raised. My mother told him he had as much promise of tomorrow as a 25-year-old man. No one is promised tomorrow. So back to work he went with renewed vigor and strength and mama got to quit her job.

Back when I was born, fathers were not allowed in the delivery room. My dad heard the doctor exclaim, "Wow. Would you look at that little red headed baby." "That one's mine," my dad said to the other waiting fathers.

I had 83 visitors the first three days of my life. "They came to see if you were [retarded]" (please don't grow offended at the use of this word, it's what she said and was a medical term at the time), my sister taunted when I was 6 and she was 28, "and you are" (they thought I would have issues because of the age of my parents 41 and 51). My sister was 22 years old when I was born and had her third child 18 days after I was born. Truth be told, she was right. That's why they came to see me. When she told me this, my little brain just thought, "You just wait. I'm going to outshine you all in every way." I mindfully **CHOSE** this path and I worked hard to stay on it.

Even as a child, I have always chosen to be a watcher and a listener. Thou can glean much wisdom listening to those around you especially when they are unaware you are there. My sister married a man that my parents did not like. My dad offered to buy her a brand new car if she would not marry him (he realistically could not afford to do so but he really wanted her not to marry this guy so he would have made it work). She married him anyway. He worked but not regularly enough for them to not need to borrow money from my parents all the time.

Having such an older sister was good for me. Growing up seeing my sister's life choices caused me to want to make better choices. It seemed like every month either her lights, water, or gas were being turned off. This upset my parents. I sought out the cause behind it so I could avoid it as an adult. Cause and effect. I tried to do my absolute best at all my studies. I tried to be the one thing that my parents didn't have to worry about. Here's a tidbit for you: As long as there are tests in school, there will be prayer in school.

My prayer, "Dear Jesus, please help me remember all that I studied and if I have to guess, please help me guess correctly. Amen."

After taking note of my sister's poor choices, I decided in my heart I wanted to marry a good man with a good work ethic and a godly man and a man my parents liked. Like I said, I'm a watcher. I would be an idiot to repeat the mistakes of others thinking I would get a different result. By listening to grown-ups, I realized I needed to be proactive in my **own life choices**. My sister choosing the wrong man caused her a lifetime of troubles. Yes, he was good looking but that's not enough to build a marriage on. When I was 16 years old, I fasted and prayed that God would send me the perfect man for me. I wanted him to be a real Christian (walk the walk not just talk the talk), hard worker, nice looking, smart, and get my jokes. Because I'm funny. And if you have a great joke and the person says, "I don't get it" – life is going to be long and arduous. Also, I didn't want him to pay me back if I pulled a harmless joke on him. My previous boyfriend got mad when I did something harmless and funny and he intentionally scared me (yes, David P., I'm talking about you). God sent me my future husband when I was in the 11th grade. He was handsome, smart, kind, and he gets my jokes. One day I was hiding and when he found me, I turned the water hose on him. Instead of getting mad, he laughed and grabbed me and hugged me getting us both wet. He could take a joke! And the rest, as they say, is history.

I became engaged, December of my senior year. I was my high school's valedictorian. My teachers were not pleased that I was engaged. They wanted me to use my scholarship and go to college. I just wanted to get married, have kids, and live happily ever after. We got married in August after graduation. We were crazy in love and he's still my lobster. I tell him that of all the morons, he's my favorite.

The moral of this story is that if we watch and learn from others, we can at least try to avoid the same pitfalls. If you're faith based, pray. You have not because you ask not. So, ask! (another choice)

Before I go: My niece broke the news to me one day that "Mama says when Grandpa and Grandma die, we get you. You have to come live with us." I learned young to have a good poker face, so I did not react (I try not to give people the satisfaction of getting my goat). Who talks like this among their family about their little sister? The next day I sat my mother down and told her, "You cannot die and leave me here to be their Cinderella. They will beat me." I knew my brother-in-law would beat me. He had already intimated such when my dad was in the hospital for a bleeding ulcer. He told me, "If you give anyone any trouble, you will answer to me." Meaning "I'll spank you."

Thankfully, my mama overheard him and shut him down in no uncertain terms. Thankfully, both my parents lived good long lives. They were the best parents a little red-headed girl could ever have.

**"IF YOU CAN'T GET A MIRACLE, BECOME ONE."
— NICK VUJICIC, LIFE WITHOUT LIMBS**

Recommended reading: Life Without Limits: Inspiration for a Ridiculously Good Life by Nick Vujicic

Love Without Limits: A Remarkable Story of True Love Conquering All by Nick Vujicic

TWO

Choices. Life's about 'em.

Are you tired of living a life that is out of control? Let me introduce my professional self. I'm a Licensed Professional Counselor (LPC) with a PhD in Psychology. Since I can remember, people have always asked my advice and I have honestly been doling out advice since I was twelve years old. As I began to educate myself, I realized while mental health issues are very real, Psychology has become the crutch upon which people build and excuse their unhealthy behaviors. **Life is about choices, you choose your choices, you do not get to choose your consequences.**

Example: A husband gets caught in flagrante with his administrative assistant by his wife. He knows all hell is fixing to break loose and he is going to be dividing his assets. So, after she screams and runs out, he drives himself to the local mental health facility and admits himself. He informs them that he is suicidal and depressed and has crippling anxiety. He tells them that he is concerned he might be bipolar. He assures them he does not know what came over him that would cause him to commit this act. The normal stay is two weeks. During this time, he gets his diagnosis down on paper, agrees to take the medication they prescribe, attends group therapy, and lo and behold his wife comes to visit him. He apologizes profusely, tells her his diagnosis (because the staff assures him this could have caused his behavior and now this is how he excuses his behaviors), shows remorse, tells her he loves her, and is forgiven. Mommy tells the kids that daddy has not been well, but he will be coming home soon. Whew, crisis averted.

Now, truthfully his wife may or may not fall for this. Many times, it depends on how much she loves him and her ability to maintain her lifestyle and wanting her children to have their father. She is not a gold digger. Women value security. Their marriage may never be quite the same because of his **poor choices. Note:** Before she has sex with him, he should go and have comprehensive STD (sexually transmitted disease) testing. She probably will not trust him for awhile, but he may be able to earn it back. Trust is consistent behavior over time. Also, she may never fully trust him again. And that's on him.

Trust is consistent behavior over time.

After being released from the hospital he will make an appointment to see me. He will regale me with his version of the story. He wants to see me first and then include her in the therapy session. He wants me to make her understand that he still loves her. He wants me to make her let him come home. Well, I can try to help you mend what you broke, but **I'm a clinician, not a magician.** He will say, "I said I was sorry. I do not know what more I can do." I am sympathetic, because it turns out, he's human. "But you and I both know this was a **choice you made,** and you did not think you would get caught. You did not trip and fall into the bed of your mistress. If you had not been caught, you would still be engaging in this behavior with your administrative assistant. **Just realize your choice will leave you with consequences you do not get to choose.** I suggest you be kind and gentle and contrite. Ask for her forgiveness. You have no right to demand she forgive you. Break it off with the other woman completely and focus on your wife." His administrative assistant may threaten to tell the company since he is her superior and try to sue him for sexual harassment. She may also phone his wife or send her pictures. Consequences.

His wife comes in and she cries because her heart is broken. Everything she has believed in and thought was true – isn't. She feels he has made her life a lie. Her friends talk behind her back. She feels like the village idiot. Their marriage may eventually be okay, or it might even be better than before – only time will tell. There is a chip in the fine china.

Television has taught people the lingo of Psychology so when they do something, they know they shouldn't have done, they come in for therapy with their own diagnosis. They think their self-diagnosis allows them to not have to accept responsibility for it. The ever popular: I'm bipolar. Honey, we are all bipolar. He will claim he thinks he's bipolar because this is so out of character for him. He will say it was almost like there was someone else in his body. "Don't worry. You are not bipolar. You are human and human's make mistakes." You did something out of character because you gave in to temptation.

She may also worder if she is bipolar because she became so angry and heart broken. We all can go from zero to 60 in one second. "You caught your husband cheating, and you burned his clothes and scratched his car and even thought about shooting him. But you didn't shoot him. You are not bipolar. You are situationally angry. You caught your husband cheating! He made everything you believed in a lie." Anger unrestrained is a powerful thing. Turns out she is human. If you are on the highway and someone cuts you off and you go to "make a hand gesture" but realize the person in the other car is your Pastor or the CEO of your company – look how quickly you were able to dial it down and **choose to not raise that finger.** People who are truly bipolar have a mental issue where something has caused their mind to go past the point of no return. Medication helps them. Mindfulness can help you. **Life is about choices.**

"FORGIVENESS IS THE FRAGRANCE THAT THE VIOLET SHEDS ON THE HEEL THAT HAS CRUSHED IT."
— MARK TWAIN

FORGIVENESS IS THE GREATEST GIFT YOU CAN GIVE SOMEONE.

THREE

So Simple a Child Can Do It!
Choices. Life's about 'em.

Good parenting includes teaching your child about choices and consequences. "If you choose to throw your toy again, I will take away. So, now it is up to you." "Go ahead and scream but you chose to throw it after I told you not to throw it again. That is why I took it away." If you do not follow through with what you told them will happen, they know you are not true to your word and they will give you endless trouble. If you lie to them, they will remind you that you are a liar when they lie to you. "If you choose to stop screaming, you can have it back. Throw it again and it is gone for an hour." There is a hierarchy here and mom's the boss.

If you always defend your children's mistakes, one day you'll hire a lawyer to defend their crimes. Discipline is not child abuse.

As an adult if we choose to be on our cellphone instead of watching our 3-year-old child playing in the yard and they run into the street and get hit by a car, we chose. We chose to pay more attention to our phone than our child. Yes, it is a terrible thing – but it was not an accident. Adulting teaches us if we drink and drive and we then go to prison instead of college, WE CHOSE. It is even Biblical. Joshua 24:15 "…choose you this day whom you will serve…" God is not going to knock you upside the head and make you follow him. It is your choice.

Even adults whine, "It's not fair." Well life is not fair. The Fair comes to town once a year. It's in Dallas. The United States Declaration of Independence states: We hold these truths to be self-evident, that all men are created equal, that they are endowed by their Creator with certain unalienable Rights, that among these are Life, Liberty, and the pursuit of happiness. It says nothing about fair. You are not even guaranteed happiness, but you can pursue it.

Corrie Ten Boom

Throughout history formidable people accept what comes and make the best of it. Corrie ten Boom was a Christian watchmaker in Holland during World War II. She and her family chose at their own peril to smuggle Jews to safety from the Germans. The Gestapo arrested Corrie and her sister Betsie and their father, on February 28, 1944. Her father died 10 days after his incarceration. She and her sister Betsie were imprisoned in the notorious Ravensbruck Concentration Camp near Berlin where she endured horrors most of us will never know. Yet, she did not become bitter. Instead, she chose to give her life in service of others.

Corrie was released from the concentration camp on December 30th of 1944. After her release, she traveled the world writing books and speaking to the masses about what she had experienced and God's unending love until the day she died, April 15, 1983. She lived almost 40 years after enduring the horrors of WWII and imprisonment in a Nazi concentration camp. People often wonder how some people thrive and others crumble. The answer is – their choices. **They can choose to be pitiful, or they can choose to be powerful**, but THEY choose. Corrie Ten Boom chose to forgive the Nazi's, "Forgiveness is the key that unlocks the door of resentment and the handcuffs of hatred. It is a power that breaks the chains of bitterness and the shackles of selfishness." Corrie Ten Boom April, 15 1892 – April 15, 1983.

In my opinion everyone should own a copy of the American Dictionary of the English Language by Noah Webster circa 1828. It is a beautiful, well bound piece of iconography. Free will is defined here as the "power of directing our own actions without restraint by necessity or fate." Isn't that beautiful? We are in charge of our own choices. Choice is defined here as "the voluntary act of selecting or separating from two or more things that which is preferred."

God sets before us good and evil, and we choose. People like to be let off the hook for their self sabotaging behavior. How many times in therapy do we hear, "I have no control over my abusive behavior. I see red and then I just go crazy." Horse feathers (https://www.merriam-webster.com/dictionary/horsefeathers meaning: nonsense; balderdash).

I taught the men's domestic violence classes at a Counseling Center for a domestic violence service provider. The men were court ordered to pay a weekly fee and attend 18 weeks of Domestic Violence classes in order to not have to do jail time. The class ran around 12 men and new men would matriculate in and others would graduate out depending upon their join date. When a new person started, they had to tell their story to the class. They had to learn to **own** their behavior. They would claim that they could not stop themselves. "When I am angry, I see red and I go blind with rage and cannot stop myself." I told them if they were in the store and the person behind them was shoved and bumped into them and they turned around to let them have it and saw it was their Boss, there would be a much different reaction. They could catch themselves and calm themselves. They would switch from "What the %$#@!" to "Evening, sir. How is it going?" If you are driving in your car and someone cuts you off and you go to "make a hand gesture" but you realize the person in the other car is the Pastor of your church or your child's kindergarten teacher, etc. – you give a wave instead.

Just an fyi. The definition of domestic violence for our classes was: Any cruel, hurtful, violent, or controlling physical or psychological behavior by a person that is intended to inflict paid or demonstrate power over another person with whom he/she has/had an intimate relationship. We had domestic violence classes for women perpetrators as well.

LIFE'S ABOUT CHOICES. YOU CHOOSE YOUR CHOICES. YOU DON'T GET TO CHOOSE YOUR CONSQUENCES. CHOOSE WISELY

I'm a Clinician NOT a Magician

The Amazing List of Corrie Ten Boom's Books

The Hiding Place
In My Father's House
A Prisoner and Yet
Corrie Ten Boom: Her Story
Defeated Enemies
Father Ten Boom, God's Man
Clippings from My Notebook
Life Lessons From Corrie Ten Boom
Plenty for Everyone
He Cares, He Comforts
Anywhere He Leads Me
Corrie's Christmas Memories
Tramp for the Lord
Corrie Ten Boom's Prison Letters
Each New Day
Not Good If Detached
Don't Wrestle, Just Nestle
Not I, But Christ
Jesus is Victor
He Cares for You
He Sets The Captive Free
Reflections of God's Glory
Oh, How He Loves You
This Day Is the Lord's

Amazing Love: True Stories of the Power of Forgiveness

I Stand at the Door and Knock: Meditations by the Author of The Hiding Place

Common Sense Not Needed: Bringing the Gospel to the Mentally Handicapped

Marching Orders for the End Battle: Getting Ready for Christ's Return

Messages of God's Abundance: Meditations by the Author of the Hiding Place

FOUR

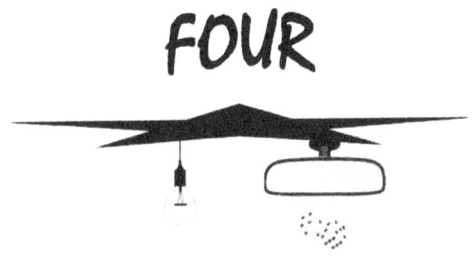

Stop Looking in the Rear-View Mirror When You Should be Focused on the Road Ahead

When you are driving there's a big ol' windshield in front of you and a small rearview mirror. The reason for this is because you need to constantly see where you are going but just glimpses of what is behind you. We need to remember the past, but we should not live in it. We can glance in the rearview mirror, but we should keep our eyes on the road ahead. It's hard to have game when you are handcuffed to the past. Read that again. Now underline it.

We should also keep our eyes on our own paper.

Betrayal or mistakes can cause you to activate the "what if" scenario. What if he had not broken up with me, it would be me living her life. What if I had not been driving under the influence? I had a full scholarship to Harvard Law School but I lost it because of my arrest. Move forward. You paid your dues. Get sober. You can attend a different school and earn your way back to your dreams. Same path. Different road. People have dreams and plans that get sidetracked. It's the people that pull themselves up by their bootstraps and dust themselves off that learn tenacity and the ability to persevere. Lot's wife looked back and turned to a pillar of salt. Nothing about the past can be altered. Looking back is okay for short periods. Mistakes of the past can educate our future. It is good to not make the same mistake twice. Insanity is doing the same thing again and again expecting a different result. Example: Wile E. Coyote.

The past informs the future. George Washington Carver was a cotton farmer. The boll weevil devasted his cotton plants. Instead of throwing up his hands and giving up because the road behind him was now littered with problems, he asked God for insight. He literally walked the fields talking to God and asking God to teach him about the plants and the soil and all things agricultural. He realized that planting peanuts would save his cotton crops because peanuts are the natural enemy of the boll weevil. Peanuts also contain healthy nutrients, minerals, antioxidants, and vitamins that are essential to good health. Peanuts are the main ingredient in packets of RUTF Ready to Use Therapeutic Food which is used to treat severe cases of malnutrition every day and saves hundreds of lives every day in third world countries.

Don't give up. Get up. Try again.

While working on creating a heart medication, Viagra was created. Also known as patent WOWO9849166A1. They originally were working on finding a treatment for heart problems such as angina.

Chef George Crum unintentionally invented the potato chip because of an aggravating customer who continued to send back his French fries because they were not crisp enough to suit him. Crum was angry so he sliced the potatoes super thin and fried them to a crisp and salted them REAL good. The rest as they say, is history.

A civil war veteran who became a pharmacist unintentionally invented Coca-Cola. Originally there was cocaine in it because he was trying to invent a medication. Sometimes the strangest things turn into world renowned amazing inventions.

An ice cream vendor's ice cream was so popular at the fair that the vendor ran out of bowls. The waffle maker at the next booth made some waffles rolled them up and let them cool and lo and behold, the waffle ice cream cone was born. The ice cream cone was first just a waffle rolled up with a scoop on top!

The Slinky, Play Doh, and Velcro all were accidents. One person sees a lemon and its limitations. Another person sees its potential and makes lemonade. Reevaluate.

IF AT FIRST YOU DON'T SUCCEED – REEVALUATE

FIVE

**Depression is anger turned inward.
Anger is a response to being hurt.**

Your boyfriend broke up with you because he has been seeing your best friend and they are in love. So now you are depressed. You cannot quit crying. You do not want to get out of bed. You are embarrassed to tell anyone. You go to the doctor and tell them how depressed you are and beg for antidepressants. Now they are not really helping. You cannot stop the thoughts. You wonder if your other friends knew what was going on and kept it from you. So why are you depressed? You are depressed because you are angry. How dare these two people who you trusted and loved disrespect and humiliate you like this. The betrayal from him is excruciating but the betrayal from your best gal pal is even harder to take. Why are you angry? Because your boyfriend and your best friend HURT you and now you feel like a fool. So, work it backward. You are angry why? Because it is a response to being hurt. They hurt you. You cannot change what they have done or save face with your other friends, so your anger seemingly has nowhere to go so you turn the anger inward. Why did this happen to me? Now, you are **DEPRESSED.**

What have I learned about DEPRESSION through years of doing therapy? I have learned that depression did not just get sprinkled on you. You were not born with it. Depression is anger turned inward and anger is a response to being hurt. Scenario – If a guy cheats on his girlfriend, she will probably turn her anger one of two ways. If she turns it outward, she may scream and yell and slash his tires and go to his job and cause trouble and sneak into his apartment while she still has the key and steal back the dog she gave him for his birthday. She may trash him on Facebook and tell everyone he has herpes and gonorrhea. She may have smoldering hot sex with his best friend or his brother. She may watch movies like "Something to Talk About" with Julia Roberts and Dennis Quaid or "The Holiday" with Kate Winslet and Cameron Diaz and dream of payback. She will write him off as "GOOD RIDDANCE TO

BAD RUBBISH." This girl is probably not depressed. She is processing through it.

Converse scenario – If a guy cheats on his girlfriend, she may internalize the anger. She will go through the stages of grief. First, she will go through the denial phase. She will say this cannot be happening to her. She will regale her gal pals with stories of how sad she is and try to figure out what she did wrong. They will assure her that she did nothing wrong and tell her that he did not deserve her or that they never really liked him. She may watch sad movies like "Eat, Pray, Love" with Julia Roberts or "Under the Tuscan Sun" with Diane Lane. She will eventually get angry. But it will be a sad angry. How could he do this to me? Then she will enter the bargaining phase of praying, "God if you will let him come back, I'll volunteer at the homeless shelter every week." After bargaining comes depression. She turns her anger inward. She will put on her pajamas and sit on the couch and cry. She will sleep for days. She will not shower. This girl is depressed because she turned the anger inward. She will late night text him. She will try to think of ways to win him back. She is so fixated on this guy that it has taken over her life. And there is nothing sexier than a crying woman pining after a man that does not want her enough to not cheat on her with her best friend (sarcasm).

Now is a good time for her to read "He's Just Not That into You" by Greg Behrendt and Liz Tuccillo. It may make her mad, but it will make her wiser.

Let me say right here and now –

The Best Revenge is Live Happy!

THE BEST REVENGE IS LIVE HAPPY.

Because while you are lying in bed eating bon bons, he is out having fun all the while giving no thought to you. Let him see you a few months from now put together and successful. Do not give him the power to break you. Only you can give that kind of power away.

If we realize depression is anger turned inward and anger is a response to being hurt, we can work to get out of the depression. People come to therapy depressed over their weight gain. They are sad that they are fat. They want medication to make the depression go away but what they really need is a good diet plan. Because once they can look in the mirror and see that well-dressed 130-pound reflection looking back at them, they will not be depressed. You cannot put on 50 pounds in a year and expect to lose it in a flash. Weight loss surgery is a drastic measure and most of the people I know, have gained the weight back or never even lost it. Eating healthy and exercising the weight off is the best way because exercise is the most

underutilized antidepressant. There are no depressed marathon runners unless they broke their foot or something similar.

People come to therapy depressed because they lost their job. I have clients that admit to me that they are late to work, curse their boss, are disrespectful and belligerent. They tattletale to HR. They try to defend their lateness by saying that "the boss's favorite – she's always late too." How about you be a worker of integrity? They will admit even talking back to the boss. "He has no right to talk to me that way." "He is your boss, and you don't do your job. What did you think was going to happen?" Americans need to learn to have a work ETHIC again. A good employee is dedicated, reliable, trustworthy, good at communicating, a team player, and has integrity.

Integrity is doing the right thing when no one is looking.

The NUMBER ONE reason for depression is poor choices.

People with high financial stress are four times more likely to complain of depression. Sixteen percent of suicides occur because of financial issues according to the Aspen institute.

You worry about losing your job but you:

Are taking drugs.

Are drinking such that you have a hangover in the morning.

Have mishandled work and have gotten a bad name for being lazy and late and unethical. A good name is hard to restore, but it can be done.

You are always away from your desk either talking to someone at their desk, or talking to someone in the bathroom, or talking on your cell phone in the bathroom, or in the break room talking to someone, or talking to someone on the phone in the breakroom. Stop. Do your part to be seen as having a good work ethic and handle the things you can handle. You can control your reactions at work. All this negativity and these toxic thoughts are not helping you. If you were accused of being a good employee, would there be enough evidence to convict you? Change the pattern of your thoughts to something positive. BE a person of integrity.

If you really want to get out of your "depression," go help someone. Volunteer at the homeless shelter, the animal shelter, or Meals on Wheels. It is hard to be depressed when you are in service of others. The Serenity Prayer: God, grant me the **serenity** to accept the things I cannot change; the courage to change the things I can; and the wisdom to know the difference.

There is not one thing from the past that we can change. We can learn from the past. If we do not learn from the past, we are destined to repeat it. If you keep waiting for the exact right time, it will never come. Jump in. Get your feet wet.

RECOMMENDED READING:

Switch on Your Brain by Dr. Caroline Leaf and the workbook.

Feeling Good: The New Mood Therapy and The Feeling Good Handbook by Dr. David Burns

Antidepressants seem to work best in the Caribbean on a beach.

SIX

ANXIETY

When anxiety hits ~

What are your choices?

If you are at work or driving or even at home on the couch and anxiety hits, take a deep breath. Slowly, breathe in. And breathe out. Breathe in. And breathe out. If you need to (and can safely do so), put your head between your knees.

Keeping deep breathing. Now look around the room or wherever you are and:

Find (and you cannot name the same thing twice):

Find:

5 things you can see and name them in your head or out loud if appropriate.

4 things you can hear.

3 things you can touch.

2 things you can smell.

1 thing you can taste.

This utilizes all five of your senses.

Name 5 things you can see and say them out loud if possible: For example, if you are at work in a meeting: Carol's pencil. Roses. Cobwebs. The idiot in the blue dress. (chuckle) John's blue tie.

4 things you can hear: The mowers outside. An airplane flying over. Carol tapping her pencil on the desk. The clock ticking.

3 things you can touch: The table. My pen. My hair.

2 things you can smell: Paul's cologne (I wonder how many bottles he goes through a year? (chuckle #2), my perfume.

1 thing you can taste: my coffee. Ah, the elixir of the Gods.

We take your FIVE SENSES and utilize them to step down your anxiety.

We are practicing the "THE ART OF DISTRACTION" to sidetrack anxiety.

Anxiety is a tricky thing. It is fear's ugly little sister.

FEAR IS:

FALSE

EVIDENCE

APPREARING

REAL

You walk into work and your sneaky coworker is whispering something to the BIG Boss. You think: They are talking about me. I wonder if I am going to get fired.

You have no evidence to support this being real.

Unless you have done something that might get you fired, change the pattern of your thoughts. Fear can hit hard for no reason. I practice the art of distracting my mind. Name the Alex Cross books in order. Name the states. Name the capitals of each state. Name the Stephanie Plum books in order. Name the books of the Bible. **This is utilizing the art of distraction.**

Utilizing the art of distraction can alleviate anxiety. You can be in the middle of an anxiety attack and the doorbell rings and it's that Louis Vuitton bag your mom has sent to you (you know this because it is the only delivery you are expecting) and BAM anxiety attack gone. The excitement is palpable.

Make a Grateful list:

Another technique that helps with anxiety is WRITING a list of list things for which you are grateful. It is good to keep pad and paper around for just such an occasion (and jotting down ideas and grocery lists).

I am grateful for:

My family

My health

Clean water

My quick wit

I'm cute

Deodorant

My money management skills

Peanut butter

Chick-fil-A

Make the list very personal to you. It is difficult to be anxious when you are spending time being grateful.

Say your grown child is a police officer and anxiety for your child plagues you at times. What exactly can you do? Is this anxiety helping keep them safe? Are you going to talk your child into quitting the job they love? They will resent you – possibly for the rest of their life. Are you going to ride around in the police car with them? Yeah, that's not an option. You can pray for their safety and rest in the knowledge that they are well trained and experts in their field. They are doing what they love, and they make a positive difference in the world every day.

I get anxiety when I am waiting: waiting for a plane, waiting for the test results, waiting for a teenager to call me back because they have not arrived home or texted me why they are delayed, etc.

I play "the five letter word game" – I invented it for me. I have to look around the room and find a five letter word on a book or a poster or just anywhere and I have to make as many words as I can out of the five letter word or I have to make five words out of it and move on to the next five letter word.

Say I'm sitting in the waiting room and someone I love is having surgery. I look around the room and find the five letter word "GREAT" – I can make eat ate tea ear are era gar rag tag get age rage tear tare gate grate gear rate art tar rat and then I move on to the next five letter word.

If I attend a baby shower and the game is to make the most words possible out of the baby's name in 2 minutes, just hand me the prize. Because of my anxiety, I've become an expert at this game. On the plus side, I've unintentionally turned my anxiety into prize winning skills.

Being grateful is also a tool to quiet my anxiety. When I was just a child the most wonderful man came to our church. He was meek and mild mannered. I never heard anyone say anything unkind about him. He didn't talk much but he always had a smile and a kind word. He was a sharp dresser and never came to church without a suit on. He respected everything and everyone. He rode the bus. We called him "Brother Floyd" and he was truly a gentle man.

He liked to sing, and his songs always had a deep message. He's the only person I ever heard recite this poem to music: (I always thought he might have written it)

I'm a Clinician NOT a Magician

Today upon a bus I saw a girl with golden hair;
She seemed so gay, I envied her, and wished that I were half so fair;
I watched her as she rose to leave, and saw her hobble down the aisle.
She had one leg and wore a crutch, but yet she passed me with a smile.
Oh, God, forgive me when I whine;
I have two legs—the world is mine.

Later on, I bought some sweets. The boy who sold them had such charm,
I thought I'd stop and talk awhile. If I were late, would do no harm.
And as we talked, he said, "Thank you, sir, you've been so kind.
It's nice to talk to folks like you because, you see, I'm blind".
Oh, God, forgive me when I whine;
I have two eyes—the world is mine.

Later, walking down the street, I met a boy with eyes so blue.
But he stood and watched the others play; it seemed he knew not what to do.
I paused, and then I said, "Why don't you join the others, dear?"
But he looked straight ahead without a word, and then I

knew, he couldn't hear.
Oh, God, forgive me when I whine;
I have two ears—the world is mine.

Two legs to take me where I go,
Two eyes to see the sunset's glow,
Two ears to hear all I should know,
Oh, God, forgive me when I whine;
I'm blest, indeed, the world is mine.

The point of all this is, stop focusing on the anxiety and worry and focus on what you do have. Focus on what you can control.

Focusing on anxiety is a waste of time. You can turn anxiety into adrenaline and get something done. If you are anxious at work, put your head down and accomplish something. You can be pitiful, or you can be powerful – but you are the only one that can choose. As I stated before, I love reading the books written by Corrie ten Boom. They remind me of what I as a woman can do. She and her family helped Jews escape Nazi Germany during World War II. In her book "The Hiding Place," she tells the ten Boom's family story from pre-war to post war including her and her sister Betsie's imprisonment in the Ravensbruck concentration camp. She suffered many horrors at the hands of the Nazis but after the war was over, she did not want to let the memories DEFINE her or ruin the rest of her life. It is a book that in my opinion should be read and be on everyone's shelf.

Whatsoever things are good whatsoever things are kind focus on these things.

FEAR is FALSE EVIDENCE APPREARING REAL

and

Worry is the interest you pay on things that never happen.

(read it again...let it sink in)

SEVEN

BE PREPARED

Unpreparedness a.k.a. Be Prepared

Do first things first. I learned the hard way to do my homework first thing that way if anything went awry, I was prepared. I may make mistakes, but I try not to make the same mistake multiple times. We all have heard the definition of insanity – Doing the same thing over and over expecting a different result.

Plan ahead. Prepare for success.

Throughout the years people have come to see me over the angst of missed opportunities. The hands of time cannot be turned back by us mere mortals.

I have learned through the years that when opportunity knocks you need to be prepared.

Reminds me of an old saying: When my ship finally comes in, I'll probably be at the airport.

Keep a calendar and keep it up to date.

More People Die in Bed than Anywhere Else.

It's a true fact – because hospitals are full of beds. Get enough rest but redeem the time. Once the day is gone, you cannot get it back.

I get up at 6:02 a.m. every morning (maybe snoozing once) whether I have anywhere I need to be or not. I also go to bed at a decent time so that I get at least 6 hours sleep. No one ever gets to the end of their days and says, "Thank God I slept a lot." Remember, every day is a new adventure awaiting your presence.

Upon rising and completing necessary functions, I immediately take a shower, fix my face and hair, and brush my teeth. This way if opportunity knocks, I am one outfit away from being on my way.

Have an Outfit!

Have an outfit that is your preparedness outfit. Mine is a black dress skirt, black sleeveless blouse with white and pink accents, and a black jacket with beading on the collar and beaded buttons. For footwear I have a pair of black Ralph Lauren dress shoes that are comfortable and never go out of style. It is dressy, classy, and comfortable. Ralph Lauren perfumes and colognes are a good idea as well. They are not too heavy or too sweet. I prefer Ralph Lauren Romance Rosé Eau de Parfum and Ralph Lauren Men's Polo (the green bottle). These are subtle and not overwhelming. It's best not to offend someone's olfactory nerves.

For the guys, a nice pair of black pants and a nice shirt and shoes will suffice. If the shirt is tucked in, a nice belt will complete the ensemble.

Keep a Decent Level of Gasoline in Your Car and Keep Your Car Clean

Try to keep enough gas in your vehicle so that should opportunity knock you have enough petrol to get where you're going. It is important to keep things clean. It's called good stewardship. If God was gracious enough to give you a car, take care of it. I always feel like God will bless me more if I show that I am grateful for what he has already given me. Same goes for parents. They are more apt to buy you better things, if they see you take care of what they have bought you. Teach your children this.

People have told me that they would take care of their house if it were a nicer house. I do not believe them. If you sleep in a hut with a dirt floor, rake the floor and keep the hut clean. "If you are faithful over a few things, I'll make you ruler over many" (Matthew 25:21). Why would you get blessed with a mansion if you didn't take care of your hut?

How many times has the fact you did not have enough gas in your car caused you to be late getting somewhere because you had to stop and buy gas? When it gets to a quarter tank, go ahead and fill it up. Preparedness.

Clean Your House:

Strive to get your house all cleaned up and tidy. Now create a calendar and parse it out into rooms to touch up on Monday, Tuesday, Wednesday, etc., then you can make it a lot less hassle. Then when unexpected company calls that they are headed over, it is manageable. Don't live by the law of gravity. Hang up your clothes. Put up your shoes especially as you get older so you don't trip on them. Three stages of a woman's life: Break up, break down, hip break! LOL! (calm down – it's a joke)

Organize Your Bills

You can create an Excel spreadsheet and list out your obligations. Lights, water, gas, credit cards, etc. Years of experience in seeing clients has taught me that people whose finances are in order do better in life. If it is the one thing they do not have to worry about, they can focus better on the other stuff. Pay day loans are the worst. I know people whose late payment fees will pay half of their car payment. The worse your credit, the higher interest you will have to pay to buy things. The interest rate alone makes paying it back almost insurmountable. It is fun to go to the mall and shop for makeup and shoes and have lunch with the girls while sharing a bottle. It is fun to buy that bass boat. Before you do, take the time to watch DAVE RAMSEY on Facebook (https://www.facebook.com/daveramsey). Go to amazon.com and look at his books. Make a budget. You can check his books out from the library or get them on your library app for free.

My daddy used to say, "You can't get a person down who owns their own home free and clear."

What we learned from COVID:

Bread lasts longer in the refrigerator so you can buy an extra loaf. Have a freezer in the garage. Have hamburger patties or whatever kinds of meat you like frozen. Milk freezes ... just remove about a cup full and put the lid back on. Have bottled water. Have several jars of peanut butter.

It lasts a long time, and it is good for you. Buy almonds, peanuts, raisins, canned soup, etc. Have vitamins, Tylenol, band-aids, Neosporin, cold medicine, allergy medicine, etc. on hand. Be prepared. Just in case.

GRAVEYARDS ARE FILLED WITH GOOD INTENTIONS.

Recommended reading:

MAKE YOUR BED – LITTLE THINGS THAT CAN CHANGE YOUR LIFE ... AND MAYBE THE WORLD by Admiral William H. McRaven (*U.S. Navy Retired*). It is absolutely brilliant. You should have your teenagers read it.

THE TOTAL MONEY MAKEOVER: CLASSIC EDITION: A PROVEN PLAN FOR FINANCIAL FITNESS by Dave Ramsey

THE TOTAL MONEY MAKEOVER WORKBOOK: CLASSIC EDITION" THE ESSENTIAL COMPANION FOR APPLYING THE BOOKS'S PRINCIPLES by Dave Ramsey

EIGHT

Do Not Let People Live Rent Free in Your Head. Evict Them.

Voices from the past can haunt us. As a child you may have had ugly words spoken to you. "You are stupid." "You will never amount to anything." "I'd rather be dead than red on the head" (that's what some said to me – LOL!).

The BEST revenge – LIVE HAPPY!!! Guess what? That little skinny red-haired girl has a PhD.

They took part of your life. Don't give them one second more.

Words are powerful. Words can start wars. Words can end wars. Childhood harsh words and bad experiences try to stick with us and affect the rest of our lives. Only we can stop this from happening. Some people take the labels they were given and live as victims unhappily ever after. If you let the person that caused you harm ruin the rest of your life or adversely affect the rest of your life, they win. Don't let them win. Take back your power. Repeat after me: I am a victor not a victim.

Joyce Meyer was molested by her father starting at 3 years old. Yes, she hates that it happened to her, but did she let it define her? No! She is an amazing woman that travels the world doing great things. She feeds the hungry, brings medical treatment to the hurting, and inspires millions of women through her books and teachings. She even forgave her father for the horrible things he did to her. She could have been pitiful, but she chooses to be powerful.

Undoing the harsh words.

When our children are young, we program their brains. "You are so smart." "Wow that's amazing that you did that, you are so smart!" "I know you can do this, because you are so smart!" Now if a stranger says, "Wow, you are so smart. Did you know that?" The child will answer with a resounding "yes." Why? Because we trained their brain. So, we can retrain our brain.

People who are jealous of you or afraid you will take their position in the company often will try to "sports psyche" you. Football players, baseball players, etc. do it. They try to get into the heads of their opponents. Football players psyche out their opponents. When they are face to face at the line of scrimmage, "I'm gonna knock you back to Jersey." "What happened last time is fixin' to happen to you again." "When you least expect it BOOM!" "I've been sleepin' with your girlfriend. Yeah, that's right, she is mine now." If they can get into their opponent's head, they can cause them to lose focus, get rattled, lose their confidence, and make a mistake.

It happens in business too. "I don't know why I hired you." "Do this again and do it right this time." "How did you ever get into Dartmouth?" This can make you jittery and nervous. You feel off your game. You wonder where your confidence went. They have rattled you. The more you let them rattle you, the less confidence you have. Just realize they are trying to convince you of something that is not true. Do not let them get into your head.

Basically, they are "sports psyching" you so you will not believe you are capable enough to advance in the company.

Harsh words you heard as a child did the same thing. They talked trash about you so you would feel like you could not get away. Making you feel pitiful, makes them feel powerful. So, head up, shoulders back. Don't just sit there and take it. Make a plan. Get up and shine.

Most of us know the story of David and Goliath the Philistine giant. How the little shepherd boy killed the mighty giant with a sling shot and 5 smooth stones. The story they don't usually tell us was that as a shepherd boy tending sheep, David killed a lion and a bear before facing Goliath. If you have killed a lion and a bear, you are probably not overly intimidated by a giant. At least he can't eat you. Goliath was 9 feet 6 inches tall (six cubits and a span).

1 Samuel 17:33- And Saul said to David, Thou art not able to go against this Philistine to fight with him: for thou *art but* a youth, and he a man of war from his youth. And David said unto Saul, Thy servant kept his father's sheep, and there came a lion, and a bear, and took a lamb out of the flock: And I went out after him, and smote him, and delivered *it* out of his mouth: and when he arose against me, I caught *him* by his beard, and smote him, and slew him. **Thy servant slew both the lion and the bear: and this uncircumcised Philistine shall be as one of them, seeing he hath defied the armies of the living God.** David said moreover, The LORD that delivered me out of the paw of the lion, and out of the paw of the bear, he will deliver me out of the hand of this Philistine. And David put his hand in his bag, and took a stone, and slang it, and

smote the Philistine in his forehead, and the stone sunk into his forehead; and he fell upon his face to the earth. David took the Philistine's sword and drew it out of the sheath and slew him and cut off his head. When the Philistines saw their champion was dead, they fled.

Find something you can tell yourself when you are feeling less than. I tell myself, "I am a child of the most high God. I am fearfully and wonderfully made. No one else has my fingerprints! AND, I think I'm his favorite."

Sometimes you just have to know
WHO YOUR DADDY IS!

Recommended reading:

In a Pit with a Lion on a Snowy Day by Mark Batterson

The Gift of Fear, Gavin de Becker

NINE

Work

If you were accused of being a "good employee," would there be enough evidence to convict you? "Your Honor, my client is a good employee" – "Show me the evidence." People come to therapy to talk about their jobs – A LOT. I cannot magically change their workplace for the better. I can only help them change their attitude and help them with coping skills. Someday when they are in charge, they can remember how they were treated versus how they wished they were treated, and it can make them an awesome boss.

The Workplace has changed considerably in the last thirteen years. When you have an employee that knows the ropes of the entire organization but does not have a degree in anything, you should still promote them. On the job experience is worth more than a piece of paper. America has a lot of educated idiots.

America has a lot of educated idiots.

During this pandemic, the real workers generally had jobs. Police, fire fighters, Lowe's and Home Depot, Hobby Lobby, etc. thrived. People still need home insurance and car insurance, electricians, plumbers, yard maintenance, air conditioning and heating workers, home repair, doctors, lawyers, and therapists, etc. Kudos to all those on the front lines during this pandemic.

So, let's start with a few pointers – before you complain about how unjustly you are treated. It is just as easy to be 5 minutes early to work as it is 5 minutes late. And while we are talking about this, be on time to church. It is disrespectful to God to be late all the time. Would you like it if you needed his help, and he was late? It's a respect thing. Same thing goes for getting your children to school on time.

Yesterday's the past, tomorrow's the future, but today is a gift. That's why it's called the present.
– Bil Keane

Rise and shine, pumpkin. Being on time shows you are dependable and respectful. It shows you care about your work. Being consistently late says "I am too important to follow the rules. Work just isn't that important to me. I'm a slacker." You are stealing time. Your loyalty should be to the company that signs your paychecks. Your behavior is indicative of your character. If you lie, you're a liar. If you steal stamps from your company because you don't think they pay you enough anyway, you're a thief. Be glad you have a job. Many people do not.

If you are the boss, treat your employees as you wished to be treated back before your promotion. Work hard to keep the work atmosphere non-toxic. If your employees know you respect and value them, they will usually go the extra mile for you. **Your attitude determines your altitude.**

There are so many bullies in the workplace these days. It is truly an epidemic. People even come to therapy and try to bully me. I ask them, "Does bullying me help you feel better? I will respect you no matter how you treat me but know there is a line." Respect is a two-way street.

At work, dress for success. Especially when you question yourself or your ability, dress the part. As I said before, Ralph Lauren designs are intelligent and elegant and classy and command respect. It is better to pay a bit more for quality and dignity (you can throw a Ralph Lauren jacket from TJ MAXX on with a pair of jeans and white t-shirt and still look impressive). Classy never goes out of style. Have that one emergency outfit in your closet that is always ready and easily jumped into.

Unless you are selling bras, don't show an overabundance of cleavage. People will say you slept your way to the top and this will make you mad, but it doesn't keep it from being true that they think this because of the way you dress. It may make you mad and you may think no one looks at a man this way. You are comparing chalk and cheese. It may make you mad that they look at your cleavage, but you put it out there for the world to see. You are happy when the person you are trying to impress looks but you get mad when someone else looks. You act like you are being sexually harassed. Dress like you own the job. Be formidable. Being formidable is defined as inspiring respect through being capable. Do stellar work. Shoulders back. Head high. If you walked into my practice and I had on bootie shorts and a tube top, would you trust me to help you? No. You would think I was an idiot. Dress the part. Dress for success.

Why do you trust your dentist? It has a lot to do with the white lab coat and the professional demeanor. Why do you trust your nurse? It has a lot to do with a good set of scrubs and a stethoscope.

Learn to talk with appropriate dignity. Profanity is the vernacular of the inarticulate. The "f" word is not classy or sassy – it's trashy. My dad could tell someone to go to blazes and make them think it was going to be a lovely trip. It's all in the wording. He told one guy, "I believe you are living proof God has a sense of humor." Mull that over.

Find a job you love, and you'll never work a day in your life – they say. I have liked every job I have had – just not always the people. I find it interesting that my female clients who enjoy their work the most – work for men. They say that male bosses recognize that they (the employee) know what they are doing, and they do not micromanage them. If you work for someone who is less knowledgeable than you, they may try to make sure you know your place because they know you are better at the job than they are. They can take a week off work and you handle everything seamlessly without them. You should have been promoted to this job, but you weren't. Keep on doing the right thing, someone will notice. I have had several clients that work at the same financial institution. They mostly work for other women. They form little cliques. They are in each other's business. It is best if you do not over share. Go to work. Do your job. Stay out of the drama. **Have healthy boundaries. Do you want your business all over the lunchroom?** If you talk about someone in another clique it may get leaked, and that woman can make your life miserable. The women who get promoted are not celebrated, they are rewarded by their former associates with jealousy and rumor mongering such as "she slept her way to the top" or "I taught her everything she knows, and she stole my promotion." Women do not make much progress because **WOMEN MISTREAT OTHER WOMEN.** Personally, I would rather work for a thousand men than one woman. Most of the men I have worked for knew that I knew what I was doing, and they let me do it. As an aside, it is usually best not to work for a man whose wife is the office manager.

Remember: Your job just funds your life.

GO TO WORK. DO YOUR JOB (to the best of your ability). Go home and live your real life.

I worked 9 1/2 years for a very specialized organization of "smart people" that had to meet certain criteria to be in the organization. I was hired by a man I had worked for previously. The first week I was there, a group of 4 or 5 women in the office took me to lunch. A couple of days later another group of 4 or 5 different women invited me to lunch. And yet again, a day or so later, a third group of 4 or 5 different women took me to lunch. The man who hired me said, "They know you are smart, and they are trying to see which group you fit in." This was so insulting to me. Grown women playing office politics over the new girl.

They were like sorority sisters vying for a pledge. Eventually I worked under one of the higher up ones and she truly was a joy to work for. She realized I knew what I was doing, and she let me do it. She was an exemplary example of what a boss (regardless of male or female) should be.

HOW RIDICULOUS IS THAT?

Women in power need to stop playing games with other women's lives and simply do the work of business. Promote those who have earned it. Do not make your employees your friends that you go to lunch with or invite over to your house for parties. You create a toxic working environment for those not in the "clique." It is borderline discrimination and ruins morale. Have HEALTHY BOUNDARIES.

Choose to have healthy boundaries.

I used to work in corporate America. I worked for the devil. We will call her "cooking spray" because she was like cooking spray. No matter what she did wrong, it never stuck to her. She always had a scapegoat. It was good for me to work there while I was getting my Master of Arts in Community Counseling because I could work 7 to 4 and attend night classes. I learned a lot about office psychology that a book could never teach me. Every morning when the side door would open, you could see everyone tense up and try to look like they were deeply concentrating on their work.

Truthfully, they were trying to discern which one of her was coming in. There was the "good morning, everyone" icky sweet version of her or the barking "get in my office" version of her. Working under this woman was good for me too because it gave me insight into understanding workplace issues for my eventual therapy practice.

Her leadership felt like she thought morals were pictures on walls and scruples were money in Russia. Immorality was celebrated. Her moral compass did not point north, in fact, I'm not sure she even had a compass. Every new catch phrase became our mantra. Special friends received points to allow them membership. The organization operated under the license of a man who liked the title afforded him even though it paid very little. All hat and no cattle. Big title. Little power. He could have put his foot down and refused to give extra points (for example: because the teen wrote a book), but he caved when she reminded him there were many others that would like to have his position. I know this because he told me. There are some things I refused to compromise on because it watered down the validity of the organization. That's what eventually resulted in my sending a resignation email to God and everybody explaining all the ridiculousness and why I was leaving. I knew if I didn't write the truth of my story, she would paint me as heaven knows what when I left. You can lock up from a thief, but you cannot lock up from a liar. So, I got my story out there.

People who know what they are doing at work just want to go to work and do their job. Good people don't set out to ruin other people's lives or spread malicious lies. Bosses who know what they are doing hire good people, pay them well, and let them do their job. They don't micromanage them. They don't try to constantly be "new and improved" and up on the "jargon" of the day (terms like edgy – which to me says you are fixing to fall off the precipice; woke – which to me is the past tense of wake; #metoo – which to me says POUND me too – which means having sex). For the operator, press the #(pound) key. Good grief. Madonna was old enough to know this.

As an aside, if you haven't read Tamelynda Lux's book, *Wrongful Dismissal from Wounded to Thriving*, you should. This statement in her book really resonates with me, "Focusing on what someone else has done to you takes away your power and slows you from moving forward." What does not kill us makes us stronger or hopefully at least smarter.

Find a good therapist. Spill your guts. Work the process. You will heal and be smarter and wiser than you were before.

**You can be pitiful, or you can be powerful, but YOU will choose.
Bitterness is not a pretty color on you.**

Recommended Reading: Wrongful Dismissal from Wounded to Thriving by Tamelynda Lux.

Feeling Good: The New Mood Therapy by Dr. David Burns.

12 Rules for Living: An Antidote to Chaos by Jordan B. Peterson.

For fun movie giggles (1980): 9 to 5 starring Dolly Parton, Lily Tomlin, and Jane Fonda

TEN

Weight Loss.

Choices. Again, life is about them. Did you know that **EXERCISE IS THE MOST UNDERUTILIZED ANTIDEPRESSANT?**

If you don't gain the weight, you don't have to figure out how to lose it. BAM!

J heard about a man who was middle age and he decided he was tired of it all. He was tired of his work. He was tired of being overweight. He did not feel well. He just did not want to live any longer. He had a wife and kids that he loved so he did not want to commit suicide and he also had a "no suicide clause" in his life insurance and he wanted them to be financially cared for after his death. So, he came up with a plan to end his life.

He was going to run himself to death. One day he decided it was "the day" to put his plan into action. He had his running gear on and off he went. He ran and he ran and he ran and he ran and he passed out. He woke up on the side of the road and thought that he was such a loser that he could not even commit suicide correctly. "Oh well. I will get it right tomorrow." The next day after work he ran and he ran and he ran and he ran and he ran and he ran and again he passed out. He woke up unbelieving. "I'll get it right tomorrow." The next day he again ran and ran and ran and ran until he passed out. Then he had a thought, "Well, I actually feel better" so maybe I should take up running. So, he took up running and he lost the weight and he felt renewed energy for his job and renewed vigor for his life. Running released endorphins and invigorated his mind and body. He no longer felt sluggish. He had a renewed zest for life.

Many people come to therapy to get cleared to have weight loss surgery. They must show that they are mentally sound and understand all the ramifications and risks of weight loss surgery. We go over everything including the risks and the percentage of people who successfully lose weight and keep it off. No matter what weight loss surgery you have, you can eat and drink the weight back on.

The success rate for weight loss surgery success is a very low percentage.

People come for hypnotherapy to lose weight. I make them recordings they can play on their phone and listen to as they fall asleep at night (note: never listen to a hypnosis recording while operating a motor vehicle...find a comfortable, safe place to listen). Hypnosis is brain training. You hear something enough your brain starts to believe it. We do it to children – you're so cute, you're so cute, you're so cute. When a stranger in the grocery store asks them if they know they are cute, they instantly reply, "Yes." Why? Because we trained their brain. The recording can increase a person's success rate, but they have to be serious, and they have to want to change.

When I was growing up it was known that eating 1250 calories or less a day and exercising would cause a person to lose weight. Now we can just get on the internet and plug our age, gender, weight, and height into a calorie calculator such as the one on calculator.net and it will tell us. Say you are a 35-year-old female who is 5 foot 2 inches and weighs 200 lbs. You can eat 2,279 calories a day and maintain that weight. Eat more than that and you will gain. By eating 2,029 calories a day, you can lose 0.5 lb/week. If you eat 1,779 calories a day you can lose 1 lb/wk. And for what they call "extreme weight loss" you can eat 1,279 calories a day and lose 2 lb/wk. There it is in black and white. We are not designed to be able to magically undo a lifetime of poor choices instantly. Clients become frustrated because they want to magically lose 10 pounds a week. Using the above scenario (35, 5 ft 2 in, female, 200 lb.), if she started at 200 lbs. and tried to lose 10 lbs. a week so that she would weigh 100 lbs. in 10 weeks nothing would tighten up and we would be a blob of human skin that looked like a tire with the air let out of it. Plus because of the starvation her metabolism would slow to try and prevent her death and she would not lose as much weight as she thought she would.

Have you ever noticed how finely tuned our bodies are? Common sense tells us that if we drink too much alcohol, we will get drunk. If we eat too much food, we will get fat. If we drink poison, we will die.

Most of us have probably watched at least one episode of "My 600 LB Life" and watched Dr. Younan Nowzaradan slice off slabs of skin. We all wonder how in the world these people got to this point in their life. The answer – choices. They decided one cheeseburger wasn't enough. They had to have realized they were buying bigger and bigger clothing each step of the way. They had to have realized they couldn't wipe their own bum and that should be mortifyingly embarrassing enough to help them lose weight.

I have had clients that were borderline diabetic, and the doctor gave them instructions how they could change their diet and add some exercise to their life and never become a full-blown diabetic. But do they do it? Rarely. They come to therapy and I reiterate what their doctor has said. "How about we do baby steps? Eat right between now and your session next week. Just 7 days." They agree. Next session they start with the excuses, "I was too busy to eat right, I do not have time to cook two different meals – one for them and one for me, etc." You can still eat what you cooked for the family but just a smaller portion. They could make food and refrigerate or freeze it so they have smaller portions at the ready. But no. **We make time for the things that are important to us**. And when you realize you truly have become a diabetic note this – you chose.

People go to this extreme measure of having weight loss surgery and rarely do they keep the weight off. Honestly, people just want to eat whatever they want and never have a consequence. Weight loss surgery does not grant you this.

Hunger and the taste of food are the two things that drive us to eat. I heard Dolly Parton say that you can have two bites of anything. The truth is after the second bite you are not really tasting it. You already taste it. In her book: Dolly: My Life and Other Unfinished Business she writes quite frankly about her weight loss journey. It is well worth the read. Food is energy. Too much food is unhealthy. Our metabolism determines our ability to eat and how much. Exercise increases our metabolism.

Tips for fun weight loss videos:

My favorite by far and away is LESLIE SANSONE'S 12 Minute Walk at Fat Burning Pace. It is easy to learn. You do not need any equipment. You can only do it once or you can do it twice. I do it 3 times. It invigorates my morning and sets the stage for the day. If I have had an overly stressful day, I do it awhile before I go to bed, and I sleep better.

If you want to lose weight, eat in front of the mirror naked..

Hunger and flavor are two things that drive humans to consume calories. Our food is our fuel. It gives us energy and nutrition which is critical to our functioning. Since humans need amino acids, fatty acids, vitamins, and minerals to live well, our bodies also plan ahead by storing them in reserve in anticipation of future needs. Most of what we eat is used to give us energy. We need energy to do the basic things we need to do in order to exist, such as maintain our body temperature, breathe, and utilize our ability to think.

Max Kleiber devised the rule for our basal metabolism. It relates the energy we expend to our weight as follows: kcal/day = 70 times (weight to the power of 0.75). In this equation weight is in kilograms. A person who weighs 150 pounds, weighs 68.0389 in kilograms. If you raise 68.0389 to the power of 0.75 and then multiply the answer by 70, it gives you the number of calories a person burns a day at rest. Because of the large variability in the size of people, Kleiber's equation does not fit everyone. Things that factor into metabolism include genetics, height, gender, age, and so forth. Usually, the taller person may consume more calories without gaining weight than the shorter person. Men may generally consume more calories without gaining weight than women. Younger people burn calories faster than older people. Genetics determine body shape. Some people are shaped like a pear while others are more apple shaped.

The metabolism of the bodies of people who are deprived of nutrition decreases. By doing this, calories are burned slower, and stores are depleted less. This homeostatic mechanism conserves energy when food is inadequate. This is why those in concentration camps were able to live for long periods on a few pieces of bread and pitiful soup. This is one aspect that makes dieting difficult as well. The body slows down its metabolism in reaction to the lower calorie intake. **Decreased food intake affects metabolism more than it affects body weight** (now read that again and let it sink in). Studies have shown that in order to lose weight effectively several things need to be considered such as: nutrient content of food (diets high in protein are more effective and high fat diets should be avoided), meal frequency, exercise, sleep, and management of stress.

Being overweight was one time thought of as a sign of wealth. The poor did not have the finances to be overweight. The media in the United States gives the impression that beauty is defined by thinness. Anorexia nervosa and bulimia have become an issue for Americans, especially the young. Anorexia nervosa is characterized by rarely eating, throwing up after eating, extreme exercising, and taking laxatives. This is more of a problem for females than males. The media talks about how female stars have gained weight but you rarely if ever hear them say that John Goodman has any issues. The nervosa portion of the name indicates that the disease starts in the brain. They think about food, about wanting food, about throwing up, and refusing to eat. There is a distorted body image many times as well.

Another disorder is bulimia nervosa. People who are bulimic usually gorge on food and then throw up or take laxatives. They binge and purge. Both anorexia and bulimia can cause death because, as described earlier, nutrient reserves which are necessary for times of lack become depleted. Without the addition of food, their organs shut down.

Binge eating is another disorder. Food, for the binge eater, is like a drug. Gorging activates opiate and dopamine rewards in their brain. Many times, binge eaters are obese. Most binge eaters do not binge on lettuce. They choose less nutritious, higher calorie foods.

Culture influences eating disorders especially anorexia and bulimia. Hollywood and social media seem to have a "peer pressure" effect on young girls. In order to stay rail thin people may become anorexic or bulimic. By staying rail thin in order to look like the girls on the cover of magazines, they are flat chested. Breasts require good nutrition during times such as puberty to grow just as other body parts do. Girls then have breast implants to make up for what Hollywood also paints as a picture of what they should look like in order to be beautiful.

People want therapy to be presto chango. They get weight loss surgery to avoid having to eat less and exercise. I have had several clients that have had weight loss surgery – including gastric bypass, the gastric sleeve, and lap-band. Only one has lost the weight and kept it off. I had a client who lost down to 150 pounds and then she started drinking because in her relationship with the man she was engaged to, he would not divorce his wife, and this made her very unhappy.

HERE'S A CHOICE – DON'T DATE A MARRIED MAN ESPECIALLY A MARRIED MAN WITH CHILDREN. THEY RARELY LEAVE THEIR WIVES.

She started drinking and eventually she drank a bottle of wine every night and she was never the least bit inebriated because of her surgery. This seems backward but it was the way it reacted with her. She was never tipsy. Her weight came back. She got alcoholic neuropathy in her legs (doctor's words) – with tingling and burning sensations and the feeling of being pricked by needles and muscle weakness. The problem was she got the surgery to lose weight but did not address the real issue (which was the fact he would not get a divorce and marry her) and work to be mentally healthy. **She should have lost the 295-pound married boyfriend.**

An optimist is a person who starts a new diet on Thanksgiving Day.

Suggested Reading:

Brain Over Binge by Kathryn Hansen

Switch on Your Brain by Dr. Caroline Leaf

ELEVEN

RELATIONSHIPS

The Language of Love

The grass may seem greener, but the dog may be meaner.

Cheating is so rampant in marriages that no one is even shocked any more when it happens. Relationships are like gardens. You need to tend to them. Keep the weeds out. It's the little foxes that spoil the vines. Why? Because they seem little, but they eat down by the roots and kill the whole plant.

Most people want their Chandler and Monica/Ross and Rachel ever after. After you've started a new relationship and you're feeling pretty good about it, how do you determine if you want to just "get" with this person or if you actually want to "be" with this person. "Get" is superficial. "Be" is for the long haul. Ask yourself this question does my "chosen one" pass the Supermarket Test? What happens at the Supermarket? Nothing. But if you <u>want</u> to go to the grocery store with that person...a mundane task in life...this could be the real deal. We can all get laid. The point is to get loved. New love will buy you a drink. True love will hold your hair while you're puking.

One of the guys in my domestic violence class said, "Since you're a woman...let me ask you something...my girlfriend cooked for me and asked me if it was good and I said yes but how about we pick a difference recipe next time. She got all ticked off. Would you be mad?" So I asked him, "What if you and her had sex and you asked her if it was good and she said, 'It was good but could you do it like my last boyfriend next time?" Ah, this he understood.

Every couple needs to own a copy and read "The Five Love Languages: How to Express Heartfelt Commitment to Your Mate" book by Gary Chapman – preferably before they get married but really any time is good. We all have a love language – usually a prominent one and a secondary one. Of the women I see in therapy, most of them have "acts of service" as their love language. She does want you to tell her you love her ... but what she really wants is for you to show her by doing her "honey do" list. The list of things that bear on her mind that she feels are in the "guy" column (plunge the toilet, have the car inspected, take out the trash, etc.)

Of the men, most of them had "words of affirmation" as their primary love language. Words are extremely powerful to them. Words start wars. Disrespectful words hurt them deeply. My personal love language is "acts of service" and I tell my husband, "You know my love language is acts of service and if you want to get laid please complete your honey-do list (I only put 1 or 2 things depending on complexity on his current list)." I know his is words of affirmation and personal touch, so I make sure to hug him and kiss him and swat him on the bootie. I thank him for taking out the trash or whatever "honey do" chore he's done for me. He usually says, "You don't have to thank me for doing that, it's my job." But I know I do. He needs my words. It makes him feel appreciated and feeds his soul.

I taught domestic violence classes for men who were arrested for domestic violence as well as classes for women who were arrested for domestic violence. Every time a new person came, they had to tell their story of how they got there. In my experiences I realized that nearly half (that's right half) of the men ended up there because of the garbage. More specifically the kitchen trash. He would come home from work and she would be fixing dinner and trying to get the kids corralled and doing their homework and she would ask him, "Can you take out the trash?" To which he would reply, "In a minute." Now here's the thing, to her "in a minute" means 60 seconds. To him "in a minute" means before he goes to bed. So, she's frustrated because she's in the middle of fixing dinner and the trash is over-flowing and she needs to throw more trash away and she can't. THEN IT'S ON! So, she yanks the overflowing trash bag out of the kitchen trash can and she ties it up and she sets it aside and finds another trash bag and puts it in the can which rarely goes quickly when you're as frustrated as she is. So, she's banging around the kitchen while he's watching TV and he makes a comment he can't hear the TV what with all her banging. "Well, if you would have taken out the trash, I wouldn't be so frustrated. If you have time to watch television, you certainly have time to take out the trash." "Well, I was at work all day to provide food for your ungrateful self." The yelling continues and she gets slapped, and the police get called, and he is court ordered to attend domestic violence classes.

Then this frustrated woman may meet a nice-looking coworker who is attentive and kind. He opens the door for her. She has a heavy box, "Hey, let me get that for you." He has a job. His words are kind and complimentary. He says he has never met anyone quite like her and because her love language is not being met at home, she is tempted. At this point she needs to remember – the grass may be greener, but the dog may be meaner – he is still a stranger at this point who is putting his best foot forward to test the waters. He does not care he may break up a family. And talk is cheap. He can talk the talk, but can he walk the walk?

If you move in with the hottie from the office, you'll find out he has gas and scratches just like your husband, but he also plays golf 3 times a week and only likes sci fi movies. He has children too that come over on Wednesdays and every other weekend.

And ladies you know our greatest fear is that our husband will meet and marry a woman who is younger and smarter and prettier, and our children will love her, and our grandchildren will call her "nana." They will brag on her cookies and Thanksgiving turkeys and you may be an outsider because you split up the family. Just playing devil's advocate here.

And men, the woman you love the most holds you to a higher standard than the office girl flirtation. The office girl wants a man that makes a good living. Of course, she looks at you with adoring eyes and tells you how wonderful you are. She loves to go to lunch with you and laughs at all your stories. She has not heard them before. You tell her the troubles you are having with your wife. She is a good listener, and she takes your side and tells you she cannot believe your wife treats you like that and that if she were your wife, she would never do that to you. Talk is cheap. You are your family's protector. Guard your heart.

When a woman's Love Languages is Acts of Service, if you want to get laid, get the dishes into the dishwasher. She wants you to tell her you love her ... but she really wants you to show her by doing her "honey do" list. Marriages that started off with real love – can develop a failure to communicate and become "failed marriages."

You both love each other but you for all intents and purposes have a different dialect – a different love language. His love language needs to be met too.

Communication is key to a good relationship as is quality time. Sit down together. Make a plan to do something just the two of you. Saturday night bowling or going dancing. You can let her pick one time and you pick the next. Laughter is good for a marriage so a comedy club might be a good idea. Hold hands. You are the pillars of your family – the patriarch and the matriarch. Your lives are the map that your children read.

When a woman asks her husband to do something,
and he replies "in a minute" -

to her that means 60 seconds –
to him it means before I go to bed . . . if I remember.

Suggested Reading:

The Five Love Languages: How to Express Heartfelt Commitment to Your Mate by Gary Chapman.

Read the book. Take the test. Discuss.

The 5 Love Languages for Men: Tools for Making a Good Relationship Great by Gary Chapman and Randy Southern.

There is also a book for parents:

5 Love Languages of Children: The Secret to Loving Children Effectively by Gary Chapman.

TWELVE

Coffee, potatoes, and eggs.

J was having one of those days when I sit in my office and watch something on TV or a YouTube video and surf the internet while I file insurance claims because millennials have taught me that if I am just doing one thing at a time, I am wasting my existence. I am a multitasking maniac. I'm surprised I don't put the roast outside and the cat in the oven. I digress. The NFC Playoffs were on. I came across a story about a daughter who was complaining to her father that life was hard, and she did not know if she would make it. The struggle is real.

Her dad took her to the kitchen and got out three pots and put water in each of them. In one pot of water, he put potatoes. In the second pot of water, he put eggs. In the third pot of water, he put ground coffee beans. She continued her diatribe about her problems all the while wondering what her dad was doing. After a while, he turned off the fire under each pot. He put the potatoes in a bowl. He placed the eggs in a bowl. He ladled the coffee out and put it in a cup.

He smiled at her and asked her what she saw. Potatoes, eggs, and coffee she responded. She noted that the potatoes were soft. The eggs were hard. And when he had her sip the coffee, she inhaled the aroma and sipped and smiled. She asked him what he was getting at and he replied that the potatoes, eggs, and coffee had faced the same adversity – boiling water. The potato started out strong but became mushy. The eggs started out breakable but came out hard. The coffee beans changed THE WATER and created something new and wonderful.

We all face adversity. Are you going to become weak, or hardened, or are you going to come out better? You can be bitter, or you can be better. The choice is up to you. Life is what we do with the hand we are dealt.

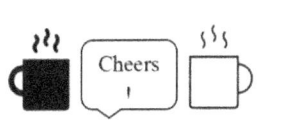

THIRTEEN

My thoughts for a penny.

Give yourself grace.

Start now from the choices you have made and redefine your life.

Now listen to me, years ago a horrible mistake was made but you won't undo the wrong if you let it color the rest of your life.

A soft answer turns away wrath.

People are going to lie on you. They lied on Jesus. You're in good company.

Run your own race. Stay in your own lane. Don't play the "comparison" game.

You don't have to take time to come up with an answer if you are telling the truth.

If you fall down, choose to get up.

You can be a victor, or you can be a victim, but YOU will choose.

Consequence is a noun – it is a result or effect of an action.

As a man thinks in his heart, so is he.

Depression is anger turned inward and anger is a response to being hurt.

One key to success is playing the hand you were dealt like it was the hand you wanted.

Sometimes if you won't separate yourself from people that are not for you – God will burn that bridge to save you. Sometimes the brightest light comes from burning a bridge.

"I don't know" means I don't want to tell you or admit to what I've done. You don't want to admit it. Why are you cheating on your wife? I don't know. I bet you do.

I'm a Clinician NOT a Magician

When your ship comes in, don't be at the airport.

Go through the mail daily. Own a decent shredder.

Keep your car clean.

Embracing preparedness. 6:02 every morning.

Always have gas in your car. Always get inspections done early.

Exercise is the most under-utilized antidepressant.

A fool can shorten his days.

"I can't" is the enemy.

It's easy to do the wrong thing. It's hard to do the right thing.

You don't taste the second cookie...you already taste it ... you still taste the first cookie ... put the cookie down.

If you take care of your nickels and dimes, your dollars will take care of themselves.

Don't have champagne tastes if you have a beer budget.

Do first things first.

A stitch in time. Sew on the button.

We all experience betrayal.

Let go of toxic people.

> Just know that somewhere in Texas, a little red-haired gal is rooting for you!
>
> You are one of a kind. No one else has your fingerprints!
> You've got this!
>
> xoxo

FOURTEEN

The Road

So, pause every now and again and take inventory of where you are on your road of life. Your choices along the way pave your road. If we learn from our mistakes, we do not create that specific pothole again. We learn to watch the road. We learn to navigate the landmines. Never blame someone else for the road you are on. Your road is your own ASPHALT.

Dr. Mary Burkhead Spencer

> Never blame someone else for the road you're on.
>
> That's your own asphalt.

The End
(for now)

www.ingramcontent.com/pod-product-compliance
Lightning Source LLC
Chambersburg PA
CBHW020555030426
42337CB00013B/1106